Beading Necklaces

With Ani Afshar

Text written with and photography by Nancy N. Schiffer

77 Lower Valley Road, Atglen, PA 19310

A step-by-step guide to creating beautiful beaded jewelry.

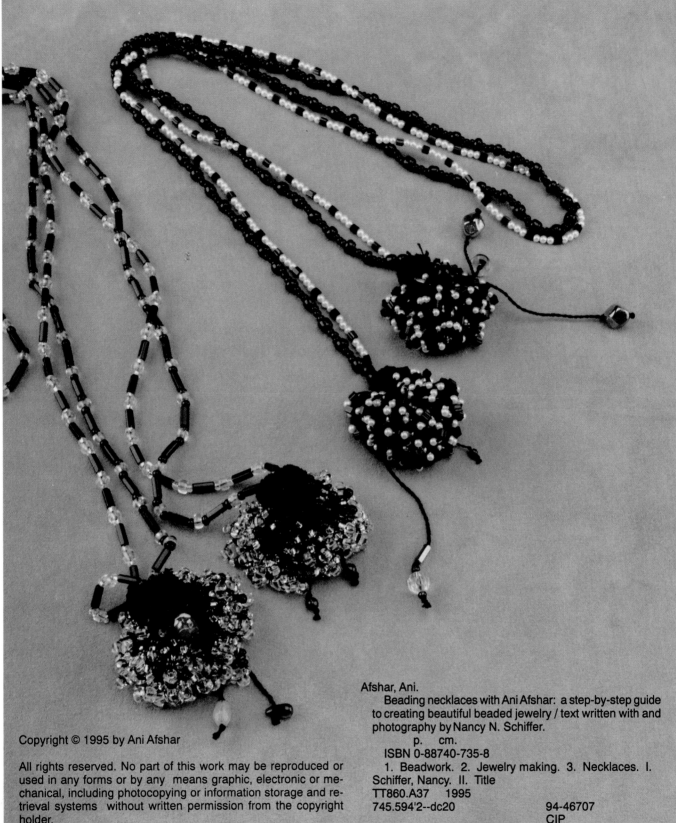

Afshar, Ani.
    Beading necklaces with Ani Afshar: a step-by-step guide
to creating beautiful beaded jewelry / text written with and
photography by Nancy N. Schiffer.
        p.   cm.
    ISBN 0-88740-735-8
    1. Beadwork. 2. Jewelry making. 3. Necklaces. I.
Schiffer, Nancy. II. Title
TT860.A37   1995
745.594'2--dc20   94-46707
                                         CIP

Printed in China
ISBN: 0-88740-735-8

We are interested in hearing from authors
with book ideas on related topics.

The name Blazing Beads™ is   trademarked as a divi-
sion of Afshar, Incorporated.

Published by Schiffer Publishing Ltd.
77 Lower Valley Road
Atglen, PA 19310
Please write for a free catalog.
This book may be purchased from the publisher.
Please include $2.95 postage.
Try your bookstore first.

L. Napier

Contents

Introduction

The two necklaces developed in this book are easy to make with beads and supplies you can find in any craft store. The instructions are carefully written in a step-by-step format with color illustrations to show each step. Beginning beaders may find the cording process tedious, but not hard. Ani Afshar has taught this system to a variety of artists who have created vastly different designs. She challenges you to take the system presented here to develop your own personal expressions through beads.

A note of caution before you begin:

Never use a cracked bead in your work, it will quickly cut your thread and spoil the project, and sometimes the holes in small beads are not large enough to pass the needle through. This can be frustrating, but it happens. Select another bead. You can throw the beads with the holes too small into a pond in the spirit of Ani's assistant Sue who throws her small-holed beads into the lake in Chicago.

Sources

Most craft stores carry a variety of beads and beading supplies. Specialty bead stores also have interesting varieties of materials from which to choose. If particular supplies are hard to find, these sources may be able to help.

General beads and beadworking supplies:

Shipwreck Beads
2727 Weastmoor Court
Olympia, WA 98502
tel. 206-754-2323

Wholesale and retail beads:

York Novelty
10 West 37th Street
New York, NY 10018
tel. 212-594-7040
fax. 212-594-8226

Long needles and other general supplies:

Gampel
39 West 37th Street
New York, NY 10018
tel. 212-398-9222
fax. 212-840-7810

Black square beads #D-1596

Queens Designs
Attn: Jim and Louise Childs
250 Spring Street #6E-339
Atlanta, GA 30303

The Flying Cubes Necklace

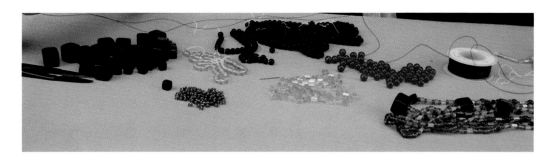

Here is the selection of glass beads that are used in the Flying Cubes necklace. The large and small square beads are Lucite, all others are glass. The brown beads are called E-beads. The long blue ones have an AB (Aurora Borealis) finish. The round red beads are 8 mm, the black beads are 6mm, and the yellow beads are 5mm and 6mm. The thread is black super strength bead cord. The needle is a very long beading needle.

Put both cut ends of the thread through the eye of the needle making a loop

then put the thread the beads are going on through the loop.

Start with the smaller beads first so that you don't have bulk at the end.

Slowly we add in the larger beads in sequence to create
the pattern.

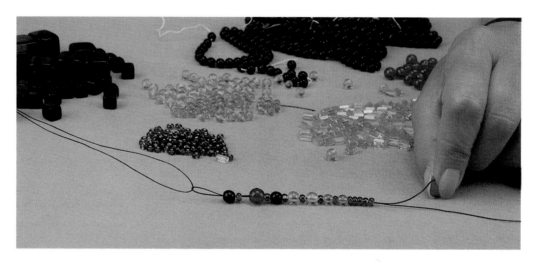

Pull the beads over the needle and onto the thread over
the loop you have created.

Pull the thread through the beads.

Start the front of the necklace by stringing the beads that are going to be the dominant colors in the necklace. We will make seven strands with the smaller cubes, and two strands with the bigger cubes.

Pull the beads along the thread and past the loop to join the first sequence.

Repeat the second sequence two or three times until you get a string of the desired length.

The middle series has three instead of two long blue bead groups.
Now repeat the first sequence in reverse to complete the first strand.

Repeat the entire process seven times to create seven identical strands.

We will be making two strands with the bigger cubes. The ends will be started with the first sequence as before, and the larger beads are fitted into the second sequence to keep the same length as the first seven.

You have to play with the pattern until you get the right length through trial and error. You have to concentrate as you build the strand because it is easy to loose the sequence.

Build the second strand with the bigger cubes exactly like
the previous one.

Nine finished strands on nine separate threads.

Gather the threads with a separate thread and go around
the group twice.

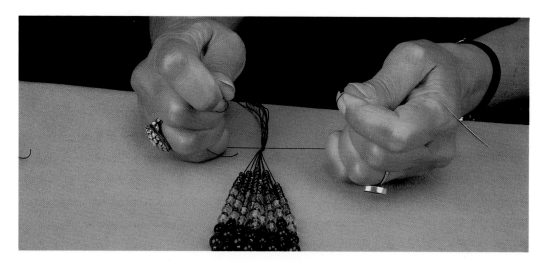

Tie a knot with a double knot.

The knot has to be very tight.

Push all the strands close to the knot while holding the opposite ends firmly.

Tie the opposite end in the same way with a very tight double knot. If the knot is loose, the strands will all slip out.

Pull each thread tightly so the beads are all tightly packed.

The necklace now has its final form.

Now we go to the cords.
Measure out ten loops of pearl cotton thread No. 8 about
forty inches long around a stationery upright.

Cut the ends, holding them taught, to create twenty strands.
Keep the strands around the stationery upright until the
rope is finished.

Divide the strands into three nearly even groups, of 6, 7
and 7 strands each.

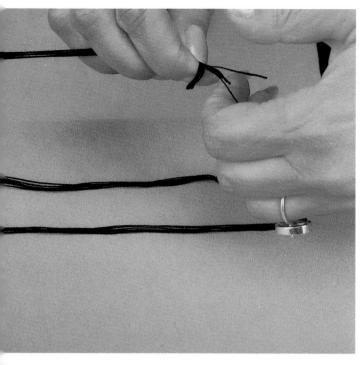

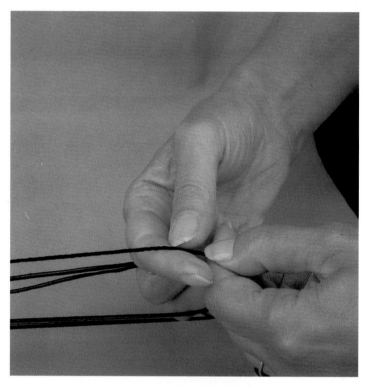

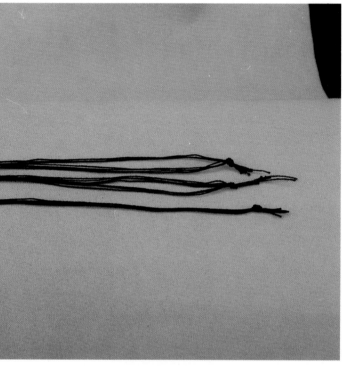

Make a knot at the end of each group of strands, in order to be able to loop the knotted strands over your fingers while you ...

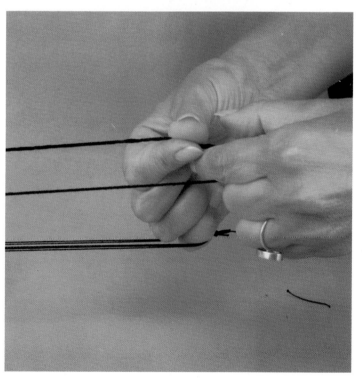

... twist each group separately in the same direction very tightly while pulling always against the stationary upright.

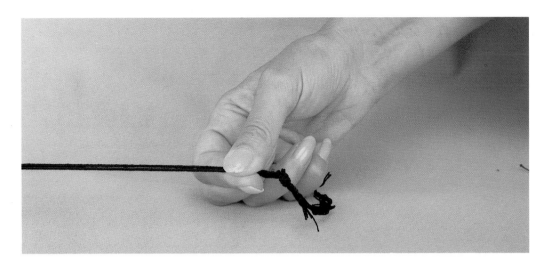

Knot the ends of all three twisted strands together.

When you let go, the strands will curl up in a rope.

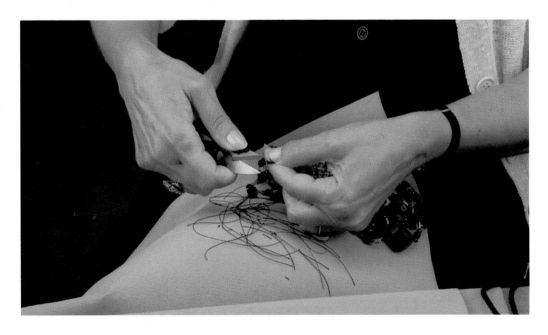

Take up the nine strands of beads and trim the thread ends about two inches long.

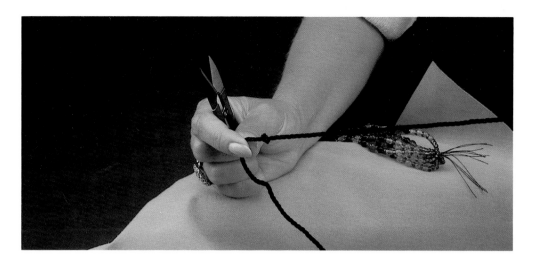

Take a length of thread about two yards long and double it over at the middle with the two cut ends together. Take a piece of twisted cord about one yard long and double it over with the cut ends together and make a knot in the middle.

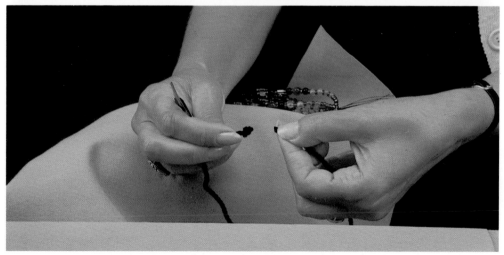

Hold the cord tightly next to the knot and cut the cord between the knot and your grip.

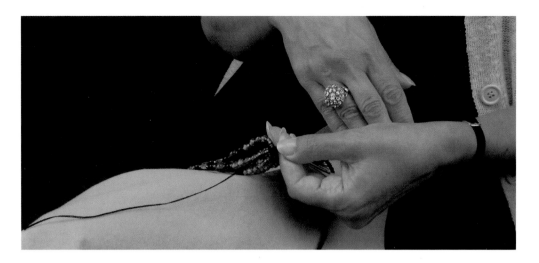

Secure the necklace on your lap between your knees while you work at the ends and pull against your knees for tension. Overlap the nine necklace end threads that are two inches long with the end of the wound cord and the doubled-over thread leaving about an eight-inch tail and hold everything tightly together.

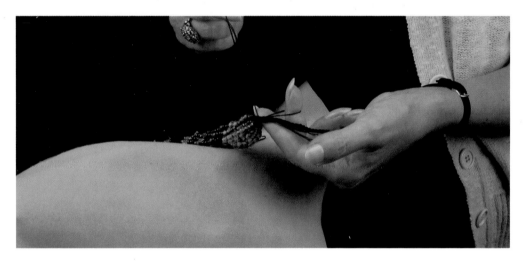

Take the long end of the double thread and wrap it around the middle finger of your supporting hand while still holding everything tightly. Wrap the cord and nine strings with the double thread very tight, starting a little bit above the smallest beads.

Wrap the nine ends very tightly for their full two inch length.

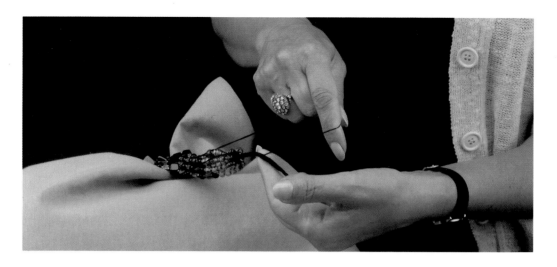

When you get to the ends of the nine threads, start wrapping back over the first wraps, while still pulling against your knees and winding tightly. When you reach the last beads, wrap very tightly right up to the end bead, covering the fuz of the end of the twisted cord.

Make a loop in the winding thread around the strands and bring the end up through it to make a knot. Make a second knot the same way.

Pick up the eight inch extension of the winding thread and tie it together with the end you wrapped with. Repeat the tie to make a firm knot.

Now move to the other side of the necklace. Take the other half of the twisted cord and wrap it with another 2 yard-long, doubled over wrapping thread around the two-inch cut ends.

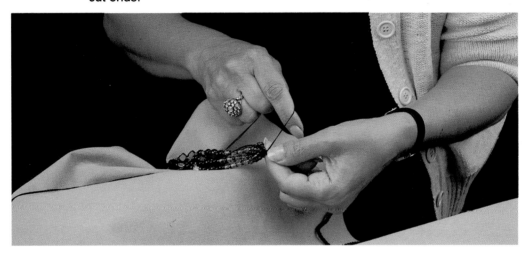

When you reach the end of the two-inch threads, wrap back toward the beads on top of the wraps you have just finished.

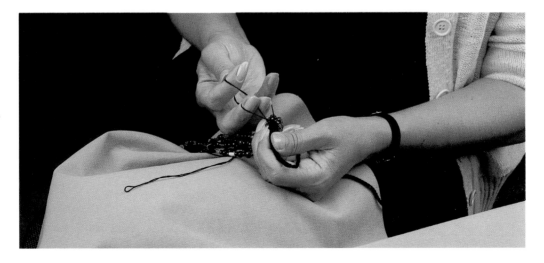

Make a loop in the winding thread and pull the end through. Repeat to make a knot and pull very tight.

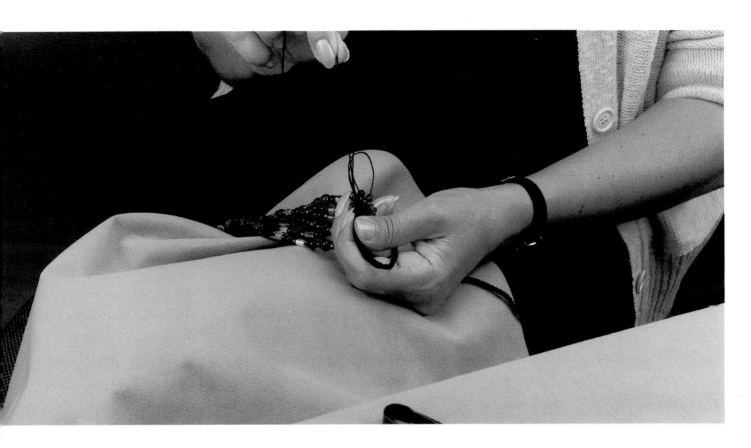

Tie the two ends of the wrapping thread together to make a knot.

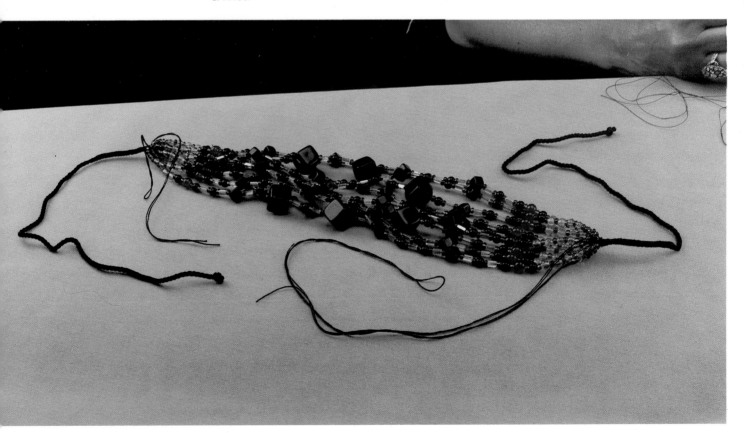

Both sides of the necklace have now been wrapped. Next, we put on the "whiskers."

Cut the loop thread that you tied off at the center. Now you have four lengths of thread hanging from the ends of the wrap.

Take a pair of threads and twist each thread in the direction it has already been twisted to make it tight, then twist them back in the opposite direction together tightly to form a single cord.

Take the remaining threads, twist each separately, then in pairs to make four double twisted cords.

Choose any odd beads you want for the ends of these "whiskers."

Take your needle with a loop and pick up the whisker beads and transfer them to the wound cord.

Make a knot in the end of the cord large enough so the bead does not slip off.

Make a second knot at the other end of the beads to secure them.

In a like manner, attach the chosen beads to the other three wound cords. Knot below and above the beads on each cord so the beads stay in place.

The thick cords tie together to secure the necklace when worn.

The Tassel Necklace

We start with the strand that will go around the neck. Measure out a double length of beading cord as long as you want the necklace plus an extra foot. Here, the red beads are 8mm, the black beads are 6mm, the blues are long cylinders 4mmx6mm, the small red and brown beads are E-beads of 6° size.

Select a sequence of beads for the main pattern and repeat it until you get the desired length. In this sequence we are using larger beads and doubling the thread because we have only one strand to carry the tassel.

End each side of the strand with three small beads which
will go into the tassel.

Tie the two sides together with a single knot.

Now, put this strand aside while you make the tassel.

For the tassel, we take two balls of pearl cotton thread No. 8.

Loop the bead cord that is always on the needle through
the double strand of cotton thread.

Pick up a sequence of two red, one brown and two red E-
beads and move it onto the cotton threads.

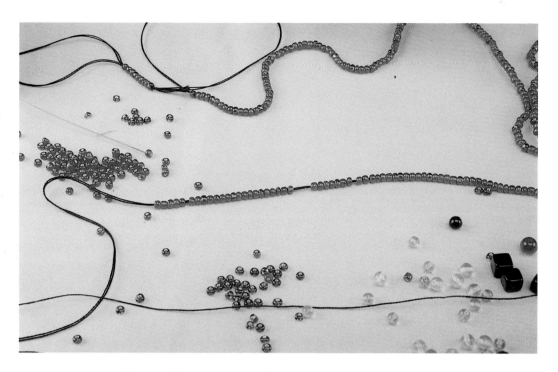

Repeat this sequence 150 times. As you are stringing this two red and one brown sequence , you will see four red E-beads separated by one brown E-bead. You can count the sequence by counting the brown beads.

Do not cut the threads, any of them! Leave all the thread on the balls. All the beads have been strung now.

Place the full thread balls into a can on the floor. In the can they can spin freely while remaining in one place. You will need a lot of thread for the tassels. Do not cut the thread. Move a lot of the beads towards the balls.

Make a small cut in the end of a 2 1/2" wide cardboard strip and slide the loose ends of the thread into the slit to hold them.

Start wrapping the beads which have not been moved toward the bobins around the cardboard five at a time, separating two red, one brown and two red beads from the rest and wrapping the thread around the 2 1/2" wide cardboard. Five beads for each wrap of the thread around the cardboard. Don't pull out too much thread at one time or you will get tangles.

Continue wrapping.

Don't overlap the thread too much or there will be trouble later. If you are running out of room, push the thread forward toward the end rather than overlapping it.

Pushing the beads forward to form a tight group saves room.

Wrap once more with just the string for security. The wrapping is done.

Look how much smaller the bobins have become.

Cut the thread now.

Put a thread through the backs of the loops for security.

Tie a knot over the threads with the thread we ran through
to secure against accidental loss.

All cut and tied now.

There are some beads on the back but this does not matter. They will all end up in the same place.

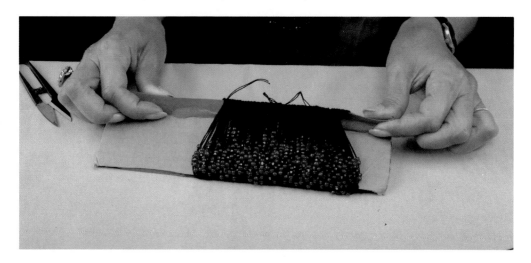

Now bend the cardboard a little.

Prepare about 2 yards of doubled cotton thread for the wrapping.

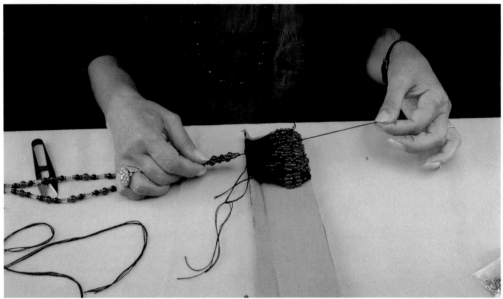

Put the end threads of the necklace across the wrapped beads.

Carefully remove the wrapped tassel from the cardboard.
If it gets tangled it is ruined and you will need to start over.

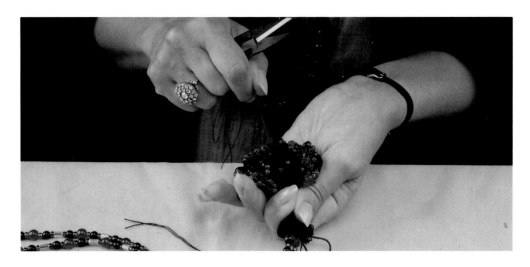

When you wrap the tassel around the necklace thread, hold it very tight ly in your palm and never let go. The necklace thread is seen extending down below the tassel.

Cut the security thread holding everything together now.

Now take the 2 yard double thread and lay it along the length of the tassel with the cut end at the top.

Change hands, holding it all together, and wrap the 2 yard thread around the top of the tassel just below your fingers. Wrap down toward the beads. Keep it very tight, use all the strength you can muster because this thread is what is holding all the beads together and the tassel to the necklace.

Go down about 1/2" and then start back up, wrapping just as tightly. When you reach the top of the wrap, start back down again. If you run out of the thread you are cording with, just stop where it ends and hope for the best. Don't try to unravel and start over.

When you reach the bottom tie the thread off by looping it three times.

Wind the thread around again and tie it off once more, looping it through twice.

This is the thread of the necklace held clear of the tassel.

Now we are going to put a bead here to hold everything together. Thread the bead onto the string.

Tie down at the ends, tightly knotting against the bead.

Thread a small bead through the four threads of the necklace now.

After several double knots...

... and tighten.

...make an overhand knot and take it as close to the bead as possible, over the other knots,...

Cut the necklace thread above the knots.

Now we put on the whiskers just as we did on The Flying Cubes Necklace. Take any beads you like for this. First cord the string:
Twist first two strands in each hand,

and then all four together.

Push a bead all the way to the top and make a big enough knot to hold the bead very close to the knot.

Depending on the size of the bead you may have to make several knots.

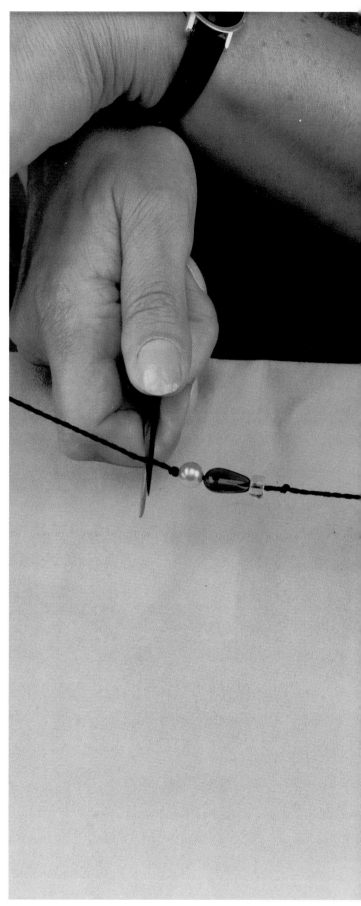

Now take some more interesting beads, thread them and make a knot at both ends so they won't come loose.

Cut the loose end of the thread.

This gives you a nice tufted look.

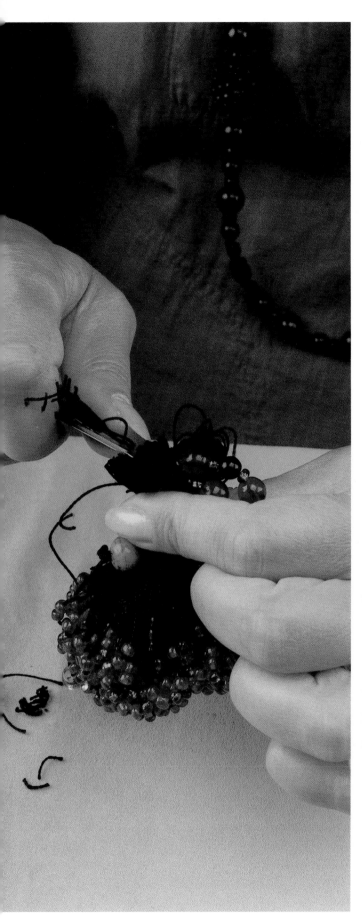

Now trim the excess loops of thread at the top.

The finished tassel.

A ten-strand necklace with wooden disc beads and green
glass beads from India.

The Gallery

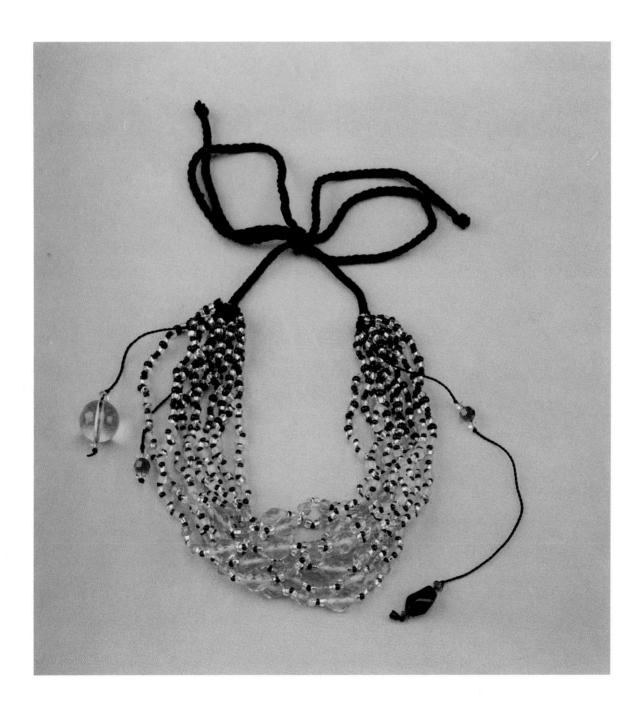

A ten-strand necklace with antique yellow Czechoslovakian glass beads.

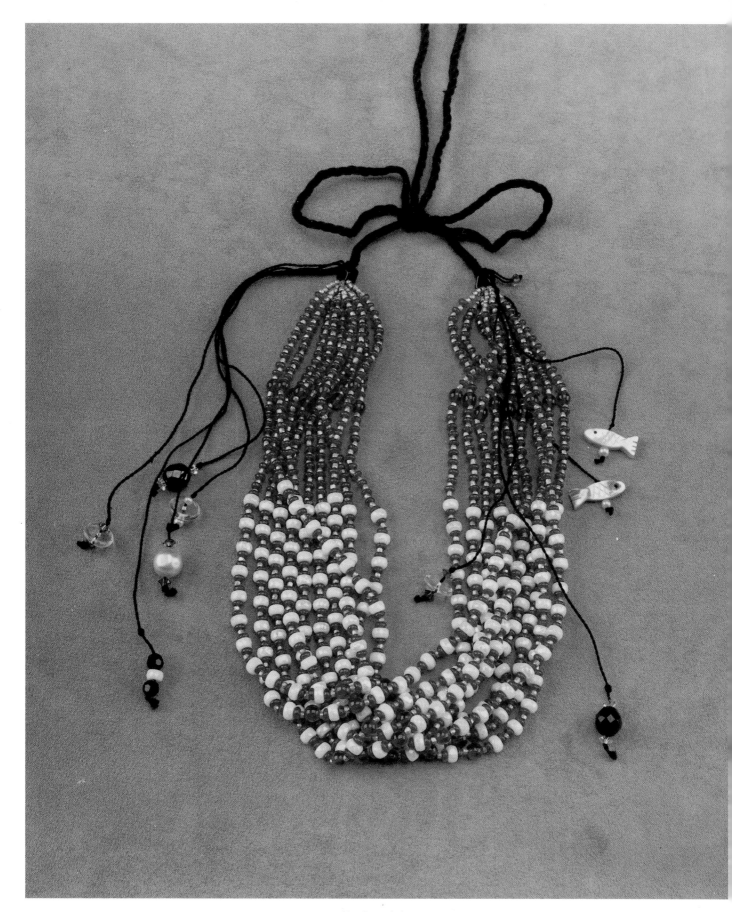

Red again!

Fifteen strands including antique Czechoslovakian red beads.

Red-e beads and clear crystals with tassels on the cords!

We started going "whisker crazy" for this necklace.

Necklace, bracelet and long tassel strand from Blazing Beads™ Medici group in the Amazon colorways.

Three of the very latest designs, an indication of the direction Blazing Beads™ is going.

Feathers from the Alburz mountains in Iran and ten strands
of beads including antique orange beads.

Two long strands with two tassels.

Opposite page photo: Two tassel ornaments

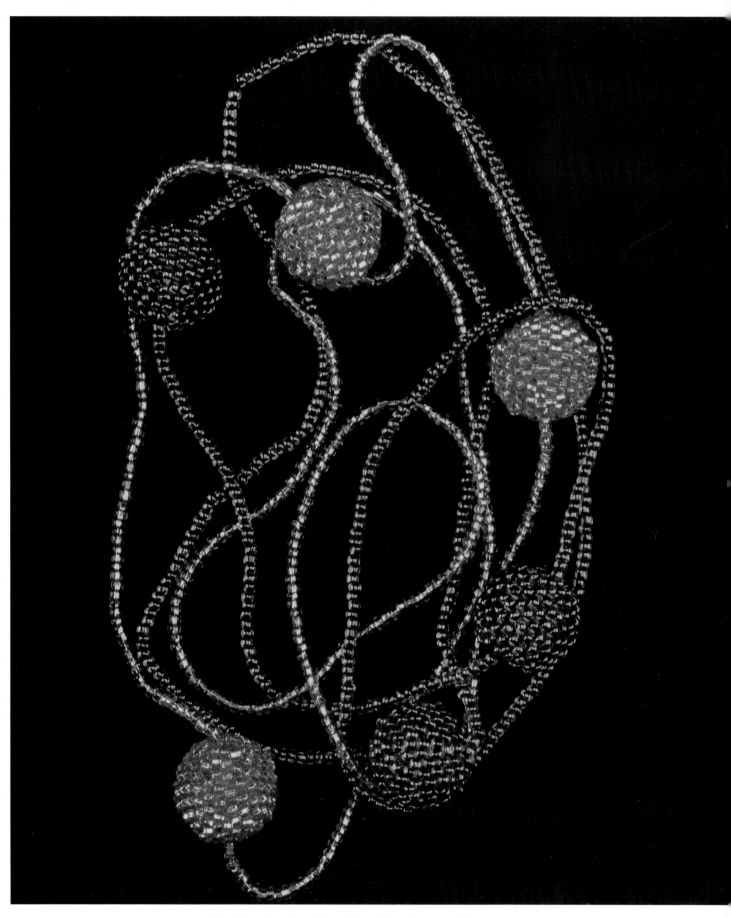

The bon-bon baubles where beads are stitched on the larger bead.

The Medici group in which beads are strung on memory wire with rondells of tiny beads separating the larger round beads.

About the Author

Ani Afshar dares to be different! Born in Turkey, raised in a Danish modern home in Switzerland, and traveling extensively while living in Iran, she now lives with Mies van der Rohe furniture in Chicago. The diversity of her background is expressed in her work, in her color choices and in her style.

In Iran, Ani taught herself to weave cloth to convey a mood and personal feelings. The same is happening with her jewelry now. Because her system of making beaded jewelry grew out of fifteen years' experience in weaving textiles, she uses her weaving skills to create her jewelry— with corded elements and color and texture choices. For ten years her jewelry was made principally on a loom with elaborate custom designs that sold in galleries which also sold weavings.

She started Blazing Beads to keep the integrity of her elegant custom jewelry designs while appealing to the mass market demand. Blazing Beads has mounted displays at the New York Fashion Accessories Expo and is represented in New York, Dallas and Chicago showrooms. Ani is available to businesses to develop new designs of beaded jewelry. Ani Afshar can manipulate beads like no one else and in this book she shares her techniques. You will find her work stimulating; together you can learn to be original in your own expression.